LO

Ghos

Prepare to be frightened by these terrifying tales from around London

By

Richard Holland

BRADWELL
BOOKS

Published by Bradwell Books
9 Orgreave Close Sheffield S13 9NP
Email: books@bradwellbooks.co.uk
©Richard Holland 2014

British Library Cataloguing in Publication Data: a catalogue
record for this book is available from the British Library.

1st Edition
ISBN: 9781909914384

Print: Gomer Press, Llandysul, Ceredigion SA44 4JL
Design by: jenksdesign@yahoo.co.uk
Photograph Credits: ShutterStock, R. Holland and
identified separately.

Front cover: iStock

CONTENTS

*The art deco masterpiece of Broadcasting House is
one of London's more stylish haunted properties.*
Shutterstock/Adrian Reynolds

INTRODUCTION

London is the most haunted city in the world. There are more haunted places within its boundaries than anywhere else. Many locations are haunted by more than one ghost.

Perhaps this should not surprise us, for London is an ancient city with a rich and at times bloody history. It has been a melting pot of cultures since the Roman invasion, and the base of government and the reigning monarchs since the Dark Ages. It has long been the most populated place in the British Isles.

Ghosts have been encountered in many of London's famous locations, including the Tower of London, Westminster Abbey, Buckingham Palace, the Bank of England and St Paul's Cathedral. Most of the older theatres in the West End are also haunted and so too is the River Thames and several of the bridges that span it.

The ghosts themselves range from kings and queens, actors and clergymen, through to the evil Jack the Ripper and his unfortunate victims. Many are of people whose identity we may never know. Some ghosts are unidentifiable because they are never seen, merely heard. Others are weird, formless things. Some are positively dangerous.

And be warned: a number of the stories behind London's hauntings are decidedly gruesome and you may find them unnerving.

In *London Ghost Stories* I have highlighted some of the most celebrated haunts and have focused on places in Central London that are generally accessible to the public. There are many more to discover, however, both in the city and in the suburbs. I hope this book will whet your appetite and encourage you to further explore the capital's haunted heritage – if you're brave enough!

Walpole House in Chiswick is one of London's most famous haunted houses.

THE BLOODY TOWER

The Tower of London is the most haunted location in the world's most haunted city. In a 'Top 50 Most Haunted Places' list I drew up on my uncannyuk.com website, the Tower made first place. If a long and dramatic history inspires ghosts, then it should come as no surprise that this anciently inhabited fortress should be possessed of so many. The Tower of London was at the heart of English history for centuries and has witnessed an extraordinary roster of noble imprisonments and executions within and without its mighty walls.

The Tower is actually a castle composed of a complex of buildings dating from Norman to Tudor times. They stand on a mound known as White Hill. This is believed to be the same mound where, according to a Welsh legend, the head of an ancient king, Brân the Blessed, was interred as a supernatural guardian over the Islands of Britain. 'Brân' means 'raven' in Welsh and some believe that the tradition of keeping ravens at the Tower stems from the tale of Brân the Blessed. The tradition states that should the ravens fly away, England will fall.

Whether or not Celtic tribes made the White Hill their home is unknown but the Romans certainly had a fortress here and this was then taken over by the Saxons. The Saxon fort was razed to the ground by William the Conqueror, who then set about building the massive stone keep called the White Tower which remains the site's dominating feature.

Among those executed at the Tower of London are two of Henry VIII's unlucky queens, Anne Boleyn and Kathryn Howard. Although most executions took place on Tower Hill outside the castle's walls, those of a politically sensitive nature or involving nobility (especially women) tended to be carried out on Tower Green, shielded from the gaze of the common people. It was here that both Anne and Kathryn met their ends.

Anne Boleyn is arguably the Tower of London's busiest ghost: not only does she haunt Tower Green, she has also been seen in the White Tower, the King's House and in the chapel of St Peter ad Vincula, where she is buried.

A famous account from 1864 tells of a sentry who challenged an approaching figure and thrust his bayonet through it when he failed to get a response. The headless phantom passed right through him and the poor fellow fainted from the shock. He faced a court martial for being found asleep at his post but was acquitted after two sentries came forward to say they had seen the incident from an overlooking window. Even more spectacular is the sighting by a Captain of the Guard in the same century. He saw a weird light shining from within St Peter's Chapel. The door was locked, so he fetched a ladder and used it to peer through one of the windows. Within he saw a 'stately procession of knights and ladies, attired in ancient costumes'. Leading them was a slim female figure whom the captain recognised as Anne Boleyn.

LONDON
Ghost Stories

The iconic shape of the Tower of London looms above the Thames.
Shutterstock/Luti

Another sufferer on Tower Green was the Nine Days' Queen, Lady Jane Grey. Edward VI named Jane his heir because she was a Protestant, while the rightful heir, Mary, was a Catholic. Jane never wanted to be queen and was happy to give up the throne to Mary. But 'Bloody Mary' was taking no chances, and executed both Jane and her husband within hours of each other on February 12, 1554. Jane was just seventeen years old. More than four centuries later, on February 12, 1957, a young Welsh Guardsman was on duty at 3am when he noticed 'a white shapeless form' perched on the Salt Tower battlements, forty feet above his sentry box. He gave out a yell and other guards came running. A search was instigated but no one was discovered, although another sentry saw a human-sized white shape in about the same place. The Salt Tower is about a hundred yards from the room in which Lady Jane Grey was held prisoner before her execution and the coincidence of the dates encouraged the view that the white figure was her ghost.

The most distressing ghost to be encountered on Tower Green is that of the Countess of Salisbury, who was executed in 1541 on the orders of a more than usually vindictive Henry VIII. The Countess's son had spoken out against the king, but then fled abroad. In revenge, Henry decided to have his mother beheaded instead. The Countess not unreasonably considered this more than a little unfair, and when the headsman asked her to kneel, she primly replied that such behaviour was for traitors, which she was not, and refused to do so. The executioner swung his axe at her anyway, and the poor old woman – she was over seventy at the time – was chased all over Tower Green, screaming in horror and agony as the axe hacked at her body. This horrible scene is said to still be played out from time to time on Tower Green.

Other notable ghosts include that of King Henry VI, who haunts the Wakefield Tower. Henry, who had become enfeebled by his old age, was assassinated on May 21, 1471, while he was kneeling at his prayers. Rumour has it his killer, who stabbed him repeatedly in the back, was the Duke of Gloucester, soon afterwards Richard III. The murdered king's ghost is seen to pace around the Wakefield Tower on the anniversary of his death.

Henry VI's rightful heirs were the so-called Princes in the Tower. Richard III pronounced that the two boys were actually illegitimate and declared himself the heir to the throne. Those who opposed him were summarily executed and the two little princes suddenly disappeared from the Tower, never to be seen again. Their pitiful little figures, dressed in long white nightgowns, used to haunt the tower which later became known as the Bloody Tower in memory of their presumed assassination (today the entire complex is sometimes referred to as the Bloody Tower thanks to all the executions and other dark deeds carried out here). In 1674 two little skeletons were found hidden under a stairwell in the White Tower and were immediately pronounced to be those of the murdered princes. They were buried in Westminster Abbey and the haunting ceased.

The above-named spooks are just a selection of the remarkable number of celebrities said to haunt the Tower of London. Others include George Boleyn (brother of Anne), the Earl of Dudley (Lady Jane Grey's husband), the Earl of Essex, the Earl of Strafford, the Duke of Northumberland, Lord Hastings, Viscountess Rochford, St Thomas Becket and Guy Fawkes. Sir Walter Raleigh's ghost patrols an area known as 'Raleigh's Walk' near the Bloody Tower. Raleigh was imprisoned in the Tower for thirteen years and took his exercise here. Even Henry VIII is said to haunt the Tower, but as a disembodied floating head. This sounds like a joke to me – for Henry was responsible for removing the heads of so many other unfortunates.

Other apparitions are more anonymous. A sentry stationed at the Tower during the First World War saw file past him a ghostly procession of men, two of whom were carrying a stretcher on which lay a decapitated body. The head lay beside the body on the stretcher. Others are decidedly peculiar. Near Martin Tower a guardsman was terrified by the sudden appearance of a huge, bulky apparition resembling a bear. The sentry struck out at it with his bayonet and then collapsed in a faint. He recovered sufficiently to describe what he had seen but the shock had been so great that he died a few days later. Another phantom bear was encountered in the complex in the 1930s.

The massive walls of the Tower of London enclose a complex of medieval and Tudor buildings. The round tower visible to the right is the Bloody Tower, where the rightful heirs to the throne of Henry VI were allegedly murdered.
Shutterstock/Claudio Divizia

In the 16th century the Tower of London possessed one of England's first menageries and it's possible the phantoms were of one or more of the animals kept there. Alternatively, it may have been one of the many unfortunate beasts used for the cruel sport of bear-baiting.

Martin Tower was also the scene of one of the strangest stories told about the Tower of London. In 1860, a Keeper of the Crown Jewels, Edward Swifte, recalled a bizarre visitation which fell upon his family in the sitting room of the Jewel House. It was a Saturday night, about midnight, in October 1817. Swifte related:

'On the night in question the doors were all closed, heavy and dark cloth curtains were let down over the windows, and the only light in the room was that of two candles on the table; I sat at the foot of the table, my son on my right hand, his mother fronting the chimney-piece, and her sister on the opposite side. I had offered a glass of wine and water to my wife, when, on putting it to her lips, she paused, and exclaimed, "Good God! What is that?"

'I looked up and saw a cylindrical figure, like a glass tube, seemingly about the thickness of my arm, and hovering between the ceiling and the table. Its contents appeared to be a dense fluid, white and pale azure, like to the gathering of a summer-cloud, and incessantly mingling with the cylinder. This lasted about two minutes, when it began slowly to move before my sister-in-law; then following the oblong-shape of the table, before my son and myself; passing behind my wife, it paused for a moment over her right shoulder. Instantly she crouched down, and with both hands covering her shoulder, she shrieked out, "Oh Christ! It has seized me!"

'Even now, while writing, I feel the fresh horror of that moment. I caught up my chair, struck at the wainscot behind her, rushed up-stairs to the children's room, and told the terrified nurse what I had seen. Meanwhile the other domestics had hurried into the parlour, where the mistress recounted to them the scene, even as I was detailing it above stairs. The marvel of all this is enhanced by the fact that neither my sister-in-law nor my son beheld this "appearance".'

No explanation was ever forthcoming for the manifestation of the weird, futuristic-looking thing. And it has never been seen since. It has been pointed out that this room in the Jewel House was the place where Anne Boleyn – her again! – was incarcerated before her execution, but it's difficult to see the connection.

Finally, there are a number of even more nebulous phenomena associated with various parts of the Tower of London. These include the feeling of suffocation that comes over some visitors passing a certain window; 'the queer and distasteful atmosphere' which made Colonel Carkeet-James suddenly run away in an uncontrollable panic; a mischievous spook that drags 'Beefeaters' out of bed in the Well House; and the force which creates a choking sensation in a room in the Queen's House on Tower Green (as recently as 1994 the wife of the then governor found herself being pushed out of this room by an unseen presence).

All in all, it's no wonder the Tower of London won my vote as the most haunted place in Britain.

A 19th-century engraving of the room in the Jewel House where a weird glowing thing suddenly appeared one night in 1817.

HAUNTED PALACES

Most of the royal homes in and around London have haunted reputations. St James's Palace, just north of St James's Park, is London's oldest palace (not including the Tower) and is still the official residence of the monarch, even though no sovereign has resided here for two hundred years or more. The palace was built on the orders of King Henry VIII in the 1530s, and is a splendid example of Tudor architecture.

In 1810 a horrible incident took place at St James's Palace, one that is still shrouded in mystery. In the middle of the night, on May 31, Ernest Augustus, the Duke of Cumberland (brother of George IV and William IV), was attacked while he lay in bed. He was awoken by a stealthy sound in his room and then sabre swipes from an unknown assailant slashed at his body. He yelled for help and tried to defend himself from the assault, his hands and wrists becoming badly cut as he did so. The assailant fled and one of the Duke's valets, Cornelius Neale, rushed in shortly afterwards. The Duke's other valet, Joseph Sellis, was notable by his absence, however. A quick search found Sellis in his room, very dead, with his throat cut so deeply that his head was almost severed from his body.

Everyone, of course, believed the Duke of Cumberland's story and it was assumed that Sellis had gone mad, had tried to murder his master and then, in a fit of remorse, had taken his own life. However, there were a few doubters. Could Sellis have possibly killed himself in such a brutal way? Why were his hands free of bloodstains? These were just two of a number of questions that were left unanswered as rumours began to spread that the Duke had in fact killed Sellis, receiving his own injuries in the process, in order to cover up some scandal that Sellis had discovered.

Whatever the truth, further rumours spread that the ghost of Sellis had begun to pace the corridors of St James's Palace, his head lolling on his shoulders, a hideous wound gaping in his throat.

St James's Palace is haunted by a Georgian valet who met a horrible death.

Another famous ghost story is told about St James's Palace.
Two former royal mistresses, the Duchess of Mazarin and
Madame de Beauclair, both Frenchwomen, had been installed
in neighbouring suites of rooms in the palace during the reign
of James II. In their twilight years they became great friends,
having originally been rivals for the affections of Charles II
and the present monarch. The two ladies became deeply
interested in spiritualism and the survival of life after death.
They made a pact between them, that whoever should die first
should, if it proved possible, return to the other and reassure
them of the existence of an afterlife. When, many years later,
the Duchess of Mazarin was in the final stages of a fatal
illness, Madame de Beauclair reminded her of their pact and
the Duchess agreed to honour it, should heaven allow it.

No visitation came subsequent to the Duchess's death,
however, and over the years Madame de Beauclair forgot
about it; indeed she became increasingly sceptical and lost her
faith. Then one night another woman resident in the palace
received an urgent summons from Madame de Beauclair,
urging her to come to her because she was dying. This seemed
unlikely, because when she had last seen Beauclair, she had
apparently been suffering from nothing more life-threatening
than a slight cold. She hurried to her side anyway and found
her friend in bed but apparently in good health. However,
Beauclair stated, calmly but earnestly, that she would be dead
in just a few hours. How did she know this? Because her friend
the Duchess of Mazarin had returned from Beyond and had
told her so.

'I perceived not how she entered,' Madame de Beauclair told her friend about the Duchess's visitation, 'but, turning my eyes towards yonder corner of the room, I saw her standing in the same form and habit as in life. Fain would I have spoken, but had not the power of utterance. She took a circuit round the chamber, seeming rather to swim than to walk; then stopped beside that Indian chest, and looking at me with her usual sweetness, "Beauclair," said she, "between the hours of twelve and one tonight you will be with me."'

The time was now a few minutes before midnight. Madame de Beauclair's friends and servants tried to comfort her that she

The spirit of the Duchess of Mazarin appears to Madame de Beauclair in St James's Palace, as illustrated in an early 19th-century journal, The Terrific Register. (From the author's collection, with thanks to Cate Ludlow.)

had probably just been dreaming but as the clock struck twelve, she suddenly cried out, 'Oh! I am sick at heart,' and fell into a decline from which she did not recover. Before 1am she had passed away and had joined her friend the Duchess of Mazarin in the next world.

Kensington Palace is the home of the Duke and Duchess of Cambridge, Prince Harry and other members of the Royal Family. It has only been a royal residence since the 17th century, when William and Mary decided to move away from the damp riverside location of Whitehall and out to what was then the village of Kensington to benefit the health of their son William. They purchased a mansion called Nottingham House and converted it for their royal use. Its ghost is a Royal from a later age: George II, who died at Kensington Palace after a long illness in October, 1760. As Charles Harper explains in his classic work on *Haunted Houses*:

'He had long been kept within doors by ill-health and – hasty, choleric personage that he was – bore it ill. The winds, too, were in the wrong quarter, and kept back the ships carrying anxiously awaited and long overdue dispatches from his beloved Hanover. Thus it was that, during his last hours, the King was continually gazing from the windows, up at the curious weathervane, bearing the conjoined ciphers of William and Mary, that to this day twirls upon the cupola of the quaint tower forming the principal entrance to the Palace. He died before the wind changed; and still, they say, at night a ghostly face peers from the old windows at that weather-sign and a voice asks irritably, in broken English, "Vhy tondt dey come?"'

Jessie Adelaide Middleton, in her *Grey Ghost Book* of 1915, notes a rumour of a further haunting at Kensington Palace. She writes: 'The room in which Queen Mary died of smallpox has the reputation of being haunted. This is probably owing to the fact that, after her death, King William had it piously kept closed up, and it remained so for seventy years or more.'

From another room in the palace the eerie sound of a spinning wheel, creaking round and round, has sometimes been heard in the small hours of the morning. The spinning wheel is supposed to have belonged to the unhappy Princess Sophia, daughter of George III, who had an affair with an equerry and became pregnant by him. Their relationship was quashed (and hushed up) and the baby, when it was born, was taken away to be brought up elsewhere. Poor Sophia could hardly bear the grief of being parted from both her lover and her child and retreated into melancholy isolation in a suite of rooms at Kensington Palace, where she would spend her weary hours endlessly spinning.

The most famous, and the most visited, palace is of course Buckingham Palace. 'Buck House' was built in 1703 by John Sheffield, First Duke of Buckingham, on a site that at one time had been occupied by a medieval priory. It was later purchased by George III, who substantially enlarged it, adding the east wing whose grand façade now forms one of the most

The clock tower of Kensington Palace, sketched by Charles Harper for his book on haunted houses. On top is the weathervane said to still focus the attention of a royal ghost.

photographed frontages in the world (the Royal Family, when in residence, live in the north wing).

Two ghost stories are told about Buckingham Palace. The first dates from the days before the palace was built. Legend has it that for some now forgotten crime a monk was clapped in irons and locked up in the 'punishment cell' in the old priory. He died of starvation on Christmas Day, when all his fellow monks were joyously stuffing their faces. Ever since, it is said, his ghost returns on the date of his death and his clanking irons can be heard on the terrace overlooking the gardens.

Buckingham Palace is haunted by the echoes of two tragedies from its past.
©iStock

The second ghost is also heard rather than seen. Major John Gwynne, Private Secretary to King Edward VII, shot himself in his bedroom in Buckingham Palace following a highly publicised and scandalous divorce. Subsequent to this tragedy, some claim to have heard the crack of a gunshot emanate from this room, which is always found to be empty on investigation.

Areas of all the above buildings are open to the public. Off-limits, however, is the home of the Prince of Wales and the Duchess of Cornwall: Clarence House, in the Mall. According to *Haunted London* by James Clark, this Georgian townhouse is haunted by the ghost of Queen Victoria's third son, the Duke of Connaught, who lived here from 1900 until his death in 1942. Shortly after his death, a department of the Red Cross Society used Clarence House as its temporary wartime HQ. A clerk, Sonia Marsh, had a spooky experience during this period. Working alone one night, she couldn't shake off the sensation that she was being watched. Distracted from her work, she looked up to see a 'greyish, swirling, triangular smoky mass' looming out of the darkness towards her. Terrified, Sonia snatched up her bag and fled the building. The next day she was given the dubious reassurance that 'it was probably the old Duke of Connaught – we see him all the time!'

South of the Thames can be found Lambeth Palace, parts of which date back to the 13th century. This has never been a royal residence; rather it was the London home, over seven centuries, of successive Archbishops of Canterbury. It is haunted by the seemingly ubiquitous Anne Boleyn. Anne was tried here for adultery by Thomas Cranmer – and found guilty, of course. Her sobs and cries for mercy are said to occasionally still be heard in the Undercroft. After the verdict was pronounced, Anne was conveyed by barge to the Tower. According to *Ghosts of London* by J.A. Brooks, the phantom of this barge continues to be seen making its short but fateful journey across the river.

In closing this chapter, I must also mention Hampton Court Palace. One of England's most magnificent haunted houses, Hampton Court lies on the south-west margins of Greater London but more correctly belongs to the county of Surrey. Here too there are ghosts with royal connections, including the spectres of two more of Henry VIII's unfortunate queens, Kathryn Howard and Jane Seymour. Mistress Penn, the stepmother of Henry's son, Edward VI, is another famous ghost of Hampton Court. Other spooks include duelling men and a procession of lords and ladies making their way up to the east wing. Details of these ghosts and others at Hampton Court Palace can be found in my *Surrey Ghost Stories*, also published by Bradwell Books.

HOLY GHOSTS

Westminster Abbey is the most important church in England. The grand Gothic edifice we see today was begun in 1245 during the reign of King Henry III but a church was probably founded on the site as long ago as the 7th century. Since 1066, when both King Harold and his conqueror, William I, were successively crowned here, Westminster Abbey has been the venue for the coronations of English and British monarchs. In addition, sixteen royal weddings have been held here. Numerous kings and queens as well as many of Britain's notable authors, artists and scientists, have been buried within its precincts. Despite its common name, the building is no longer an abbey but bears the official title of Collegiate Church of St Peter at Westminster.

Spectral monks or nuns are the staple ghosts of old ecclesiastical buildings and it would be surprising if Westminster Abbey was unable to offer one or two of its own. Shadowy cowled figures have been encountered in the cloisters and on one occasion a policeman on night duty saw a monk hurry towards the locked western entrance and pass through it as if it was air. Puzzled and a little alarmed, the constable approached the door but then noticed a procession of men, their heads bowed and their arms folded, walking towards him, two by two, their sandalled feet making no sound on the flagstoned path. He stood in amazement as they too passed through the solid door. Checking to make sure the heavy oak door was indeed still firmly secured, he detected the sound of 'sweet and plaintive' music coming from within. A moment later all was quiet.

'Father Benedictus' is, however, the best-known ghostly monk of Westminster Abbey. Father Benedictus is a rare example of a ghost which appears to be not only aware of its surroundings but also interacts with people. His haughty demeanour implies that he doesn't approve of the modern world, nor of the tourists who now crowd the abbey's cloisters. A young woman sitting quietly waiting for Evensong to begin got a good look at Father Benedictus and told reporters about her sighting:

'I became aware that someone was staring at me very intently,' she said. 'I turned round and looked into the eyes of a Benedictine monk. He was standing with his hands hidden in the sleeves of his habit and his cowl half back from his head. He swept the assembly with a very contemptuous glance then looked straight at me again. Slowly he walked backwards, pausing at intervals, scornfully looking at people in the transept. Finally he disappeared through the wall in a southward direction. The whole appearance lasted twenty-five minutes.'

Others who have seen him have described Father Benedictus as having a hooked nose and prominent but deep-set brown eyes. His most common time for manifesting in the cloisters is between five and six o'clock in the evening. He has been known to speak to visitors. One witness said he seemed to speaking a kind of 'Elizabethan English'; others failed to

Magnificent Westminster Abbey is haunted by the scornful Father Benedictus, among other ghosts. Shutterstock/iolya

notice any peculiarities in his mode of speech. Another witness noted that he was walking about an inch off the ground, the flagstones presumably having been worn down by that amount over the intervening centuries.

According to legend, Father Benedictus was killed in the abbey during the reign of Henry VIII. He was murdered by thieves whom he surprised in the Chapel. They ran him through with a lance and then made off with the pyx.

The most poignant ghost of Westminster Abbey is the one seen near the Tomb of the Unknown Warrior. The monument was erected to honour all those who died fighting during the First World War, particularly those who lie in unmarked graves. The apparition of a young man in the khaki uniform of an infantryman of the Great War has been seen standing by the monument, his head bowed as if in mourning. Some have seen him standing with one arm outstretched, his eyes 'full of a strange pleading', as if he is beseeching somebody to do something he cannot now articulate.

In St Paul's Cathedral, All Souls Chapel was renamed the Kitchener Memorial Chapel and rededicated to the memory of soldiers who died during the First World War. From time to time the apparition of an elderly cleric in an old-fashioned gown has been known to manifest in this chapel. He stands whistling a tuneless dirge and then turns and walks through a wall, always in the same place. Some years ago, during repairs, a small door was found concealed behind the plasterwork at the place where the ghost was seen to vanish. The doorway opened onto a narrow corkscrew staircase that led up to a passage built into the inner cupola of the dome.

There is a tale, too, of a ghostly woman who is seen to kneel in one of the aisles, not praying but casting about as if searching for something. Anyone who asks her if they can be of help is invariably startled by the woman suddenly disappearing into thin air. More bizarre is the mysterious 'great black cloud' that was allegedly encountered by two tourists in 1899. They said that as they were making their way down the central aisle, the shadowy thing burst out of the ground in front of them and hovered twenty feet in the air above them. The couple were convinced that the cloud was animated with some form of horrible life. Before they had time to react to the looming menace, it had vanished.

Christopher Wren's masterpiece, St Paul's Cathedral, is haunted by a whistling clergyman and two other unusual spooks.
Shutterstock/Dan Breckwoldt

Westminster Abbey and St Paul's Cathedral are London's most magnificent places of worship but many of its smaller churches have haunted reputations, too. The Church of St James Garlickhythe, off Upper Thames Street, is another Wren church, replacing a medieval building damaged during the Great Fire of 1666. Until fairly recently the vestibule of the church housed a most unusual artefact, a glass-fronted coffin containing the mummified body of a man. The identity of the corpse is unknown but this unusual and expensive mode of burial suggests he had been a man of importance. He was long nicknamed 'Old Jimmy Garlickhythe'.

During the First World War, a bomb dropped by a Zeppelin narrowly missed the church and in thanksgiving a 'Bomb Sermon' was instituted here. Perhaps this is why, when another German bomb crashed through the roof during the next World War, it failed to explode. Nevertheless, this desecration disturbed the rest of 'Old Jimmy Garlickhythe', and his ghost has been seen in the church since the incident took place in 1942. One of the first sightings occurred when an American visitor was looking round St James's with her two sons. Her eldest boy was horrified to see what he described as an incredibly emaciated man staring down at him from a stairway leading to the balcony. He said the figure was wrapped in a shroud and had his hands crossed on his chest like a mummy. There were several other sightings of Jimmy's corpse in apparition form, but not since he has been taken away from view and re-interred in the tower.

A phantom pussycat haunted All Hallows-by-the-Tower in Byward Street. All Hallows was not as fortunate as St James's and suffered badly from bomb damage during the Second World War. Prior to its post-war restoration, there were a number of reports of a ghostly cat being seen about the church. When he was a choirboy a Mr Reginald Hill watched as the spectral white animal crept around the organ loft. He was learning a new piece with the organist, who became increasingly irritated as the young Reginald kept trying to point out the cat, which only he could see. At one point it was perched complacently on the organ stool, jumping down and vanishing into thin air when the music master sat down.

It is believed that the ghost was of a white Persian owned by a Miss Rist, the organist in All Hallows during the mid 19th century. Miss Rist was a well-known animal lover, who made

Animal lover Miss Rist scatters sawdust to help horses gain a better purchase during snowy weather. Miss Rist's favourite animal, a white Persian cat, haunted a London church long after its death.

it her duty on snowy or icy mornings to lay down sawdust so that horses hauling deliveries up Tower Hill wouldn't slip and suffer injuries. Everywhere she went, her pet cat followed her, and it would sit by her as she played the organ. When it died, she asked that the cat be buried in consecrated ground in the churchyard but the request was refused. Perhaps this is why the phantom Persian haunted All Hallows for at least a century following its death.

The Church of St Magnus the Martyr near London Bridge is another designed by Wren to replace one destroyed by the Great Fire; indeed, the old St Magnus's was the first church to be consumed by the flames. Its quiet ghost is of a cowled figure which emanates an atmosphere of gloom. It is most often seen standing near the tomb of Miles Coverdale, Bishop of Exeter (the man who first translated the Bible into English), and it has therefore been suggested that the melancholy spirit may be Coverdale himself.

Rather more dramatic are the ghosts which tradition claims as haunting the churchyard of Greyfriars in Newgate Street. Greyfriars was an important house of Franciscan monks, based around the now ruined Christ Church. Hundreds of nobles were buried here, including Queen Isabella, the 'She-Wolf of France', who deposed her husband, Edward II, and had him murdered. After her own death, she was interred at Greyfriars, with, rather unbelievably, her dead husband's heart on her chest. Lady Margaret Hungerford, who poisoned her husband in the 16th century and was hanged for it, is also buried here. Both women haunt the churchyard and one fanciful account suggests that they became bitter rivals after death and engage in a kind of paranormal cat-fight among the graves.

A more gentle presence in Greyfriars is the so-called 'Holy Maid of Kent', whose real name was Elizabeth Barton. Elizabeth claimed to have the gift of prophecy and foolishly prophesied the downfall of the kingdom if King Henry VIII divorced Catherine of Aragon. She was burnt alive in 1534 for her temerity. In addition to the female phantoms of Greyfriars churchyard, a brown-clad monk and a spectral dog have also been glimpsed by people enjoying the tranquil little garden here.

The sighting of a possible ghost in the Catholic Westminster Cathedral led to the police being called. A sacristan on night duty saw a 'black-clad figure' creeping down the aisle towards the high altar, where it vanished. Assuming it was an intruder, the sacristan dialled 999 and the police carried out an extensive search both inside and outside the cathedral but without finding anyone. Their sniffer dogs failed to pick up any scent. The embarrassed witness realised that he may well have seen a ghost, possibly of a monk.

The church tower of St Magnus the Martyr. The ghost of St Magnus's has been
tentatively identified as being of a 16th-century bishop.
Shutterstock/Neil Lang

Without doubt one of London's most haunted churches is St Bartholomew the Great in Smithfield. The monk-like figure haunting St Bart's is thought to be of Rahere, who founded the original St Bartholomew's Hospital, of which the church was formerly a part. Rahere was a monk, scholar and court favourite of King Henry I. He is said to have been a great wit and has been described as Henry's jester. After contracting malaria on a pilgrimage to Rome, he made an oath that if God would spare him he would found a hospital for the poor in gratitude. He claimed that St Bartholomew appeared to him in a dream and told him where to build it. Rahere recovered and returned to London, founding the hospital in 1123.

The ghost haunts the vicinity of Rahere's impressive tomb in the church and has therefore been identified with him. In her *Ghosts Vivisected*, Anna Stirling spoke to a former rector's wife who saw the ghost on more than one occasion. She writes: 'Mrs Sandwith was arranging flowers on the altar when she heard a faint sound behind her and, looking round, she saw the figure of a monk standing at a little distance. His cowl was drawn over his head and his face was invisible. She spoke to him, but he did not answer, and he glided away noiselessly into the vestry. She at once followed, but to her astonishment found no one there.'

This took place one Christmas Eve. During the Christmas Day service, her husband, the Revd W Sandwith, was astonished to see, 'on the capital of one of the pillars adjacent, apparently looking down at me … a monk's face encircled by a cowl'. He was so amazed that he was barely able to get through his reading of the service. On another occasion, Mr Sandwith saw a different apparition, which he described as 'evidently a Divine of the Reformation period', perched up in the pulpit and apparently delivering a bombastic but entirely silent sermon to an invisible congregation.

The ghost of a little man in antiquated dress, including an old-fashioned hat cocked at a rakish angle, has also been seen in the church. It has been suggested that this is the satirical artist of the 18th-century, William Hogarth, who was baptised in St Bartholomew the Great and who made it his regular place of worship. The legendary ghost-hunter Elliott O'Donnell recorded two other, somewhat vague, supernatural presences in this venerable church: a luminous white shape in the central aisle and a shadowy shape emanating evil which creeps down one of the ambulatories.

The exterior of St Bartholomew the Great is also haunted, for nearby are the sites of numerous executions carried out during the turbulent years of the 16th century. Here Henry VIII had burnt alive anyone who dared refute his right to instigate the Reformation. When the devoutly Catholic Queen Mary took the throne, she revenged herself on those who had helped found the Church of England by burning Protestant Martyrs. After she was deposed by her Protestant sister Elizabeth I, it was the turn of yet more Catholics, plus numerous other plotters and criminals, to meet their end in Smithfield.

Many of these unfortunates were tied to stakes facing the eastern end of St Bartholomew's. There are reports of eerie cries and screams being heard where the executions took place, and these are occasionally accompanied by – horrible though it is to tell – the stench of burning flesh.

The Priory Church of St Bartholomew the Great is arguably London's most haunted place of worship. Shutterstock/Kiev.Victor

PHANTOMS IN THE FOOTLIGHTS

London's West End is celebrated as a cultural powerhouse, sharing with Broadway in New York a worldwide reputation for staging the very best theatrical productions. Many of London's theatres are of considerable age, with a long and unbeatable history of great performances by great stars. Whether it is due to their rich history or to the strong and remarkable personalities associated with them, the fact remains that a surprising number of these playhouses have a reputation for ghosts.

When Sir Patrick Stewart was starring in a 2009 production of Samuel Beckett's *Waiting For Godot* at the Theatre Royal, Haymarket, he became momentarily distracted and fluffed his line. In the interval, his co-star, Sir Ian McKellen, asked Stewart what had thrown him. Stewart replied: 'I just saw a ghost. On stage in Act One.' The actor had noticed a figure in antiquated costume intently watching their performance from the back of the stage. Almost as soon as he saw it, the apparition vanished.

Staff at the theatre were quick to reassure Sir Patrick that he wasn't going crazy, and that he had almost certainly seen the well-known ghost of the Haymarket, John Buckstone. Buckstone was actor-manager at the Haymarket in the 19th century and had been a close friend of Charles Dickens. His ghostly appearances began a year after his death. It was as if he simply couldn't bear to be apart from the theatre he loved. Originally a comic actor, Buckstone tends to visit when comedies are running and his appearances are always taken as a sign of approval. *Waiting for Godot* is not usually described as a comedy but does feature some knockabout action and has a darkly comic vein running through it.

In 2009 a director of the Haymarket, Nigel Everett, said: 'Patrick told us all about it. He was stunned. I would not say frightened, but I would say impressed. I think Buckstone appears when he appreciates things. We view it as a positive thing.'

Sir Patrick Stewart, who saw the ghost of the Theatre Royal, Haymarket, in the midst of a performance.
Shutterstock/DFree

Mr Everett added that to his knowledge the last time Buckstone had been seen by an actor on stage was in the mid-1990s, when Fiona Fullerton noticed him during the performance of an Oscar Wilde play. Other famous actors to have seen Buckstone's ghost include Margaret Rutherford and Donald Sinden.

Another recent ghost sighting took place at the Adelphi Theatre on The Strand, this time over the very modern medium of Skype. In 2013 comedian Jason Manford was performing at the Adelphi and later learnt that he had been given the so-called 'haunted dressing room'. He was talking to his three-year-old daughter over his webcam when she suddenly blurted out: 'Daddy, what is that man doing behind you?'

Since no one else was in the room, the confused Manford asked his little girl what the man looked like. She replied: 'He's a soldier.'

When he spoke to the management about the spooky incident, they told Manford the famous ghost story of the Adelphi. In 1897 Victorian heart-throb actor William Terriss was stabbed to death by a jealous understudy when he arrived at the theatre. According to the story told to Jason Manford, Terris was murdered on the night he was due to appear in a play called *The Secret Service*, in which he would have been dressed as a lieutenant in the American Army – a soldier, in other words.

Other reports of the apparition describe Terriss as wearing 'a flowing tie and a sombrero hat'. He has been seen in various parts of the theatre, including on the stage, and also by the back entrance to the theatre in Bull Inn Court, where he was killed. The actor Peter Wyngarde reported strange goings-on in 'the haunted dressing room', including objects being moved about. Some blamed these on the ghost of William Terriss but Wyngarde was also told that actor and composer Ivor Novello haunted the Adelphi and that his restless spirit might have been responsible.

For reasons which remain obscure, William Terriss also haunts nearby Covent Garden Underground Station. Here he has been described as 'a tall distinguished-looking spectre … wearing a grey suit, old-fashioned collar and white gloves'. Intriguingly, this would fairly accurately describe the grey army uniform he would have worn on stage at the Adelphi. One member of the London Transport staff got the fright of his life when a white-gloved hand reached out of the darkness and touched him with icy fingers. Another staff member, back in the 1970s, claimed to have seen the apparition at least forty times and said that he had got quite used to it.

(A remarkable number of ghost sightings have been reported from the network of Tube stations. To learn more, you might like to pick up a copy of *London Underground Ghost Stories* by Jill Armitage, also published by Bradwell Books.)

Covent Garden Underground Station is the surprising haunt of murdered actor
William Terriss, who also haunts the Adelphi Theatre.
Shutterstock/Cedric Weber

The Theatre Royal, Drury Lane, was first constructed in 1663, making this the oldest site in London used continuously as a theatre. Three more buildings have stood here since that time, however. In 1791 the playwright Richard Brinsley Sheridan bought Drury Lane (as the theatre is usually known) and invested heavily in a brand new building, which unfortunately burnt to the ground fifteen years later. He is said to have watched the conflagration from a coffee shop on the opposite side of the street. 'Can't a man enjoy a drink by his own fireside?' he coolly quipped as he watched thousands of pounds worth of investment go up in flames. The current theatre is the one that replaced it, constructed in 1812.

At least two of the ghosts of Drury Lane appear to pre-date the current building but since the location has so long been occupied by a theatre, this should not necessarily invalidate them. The phantom known as 'The Man in Grey' has been seen making his way across the Upper Circle, usually in daylight, disappearing through the wall at the far end. He wears a grey riding cloak with a tricorn hat perched atop his powdered wig. Like the ghost of the Theatre Royal, Haymarket, his appearances are believed to grant favour on a production, guaranteeing a long run. No one knows the identity of The Man in Grey but he is presumed to be connected to another mystery. In the 1840s, during alteration work, a cavity was found in the wall near where the ghost now begins his stroll. Inside was a huddled-up skeleton, a dagger between its ribs. Here then was evidence of a past murder but one for which no possible history has ever come to light. The Man in Grey must remain anonymous.

Joseph Braddock, in his *Haunted Houses*, records another strange haunting at Drury Lane, one which occurred on stage in front of hundreds of people. An American actress, Betty Jo Jones, joined the cast of *Oklahoma* to take on the comic role of 'Ado Annie'. Initially this was not a happy experience. Try as she might, she was unable to succeed in her role and failed to get the laughs. Then, during one performance, something very odd happened.

Writes Mr Braddock: 'One night she was playing a scene in which two actors were on the stage with her. Suddenly she felt a gentle tug at her skirt. She looked round, but neither of the men, as the scene demanded, were near enough to have touched her. Now she was aware of two hands upon her shoulders, gently but firmly forcing her down stage and guiding her body into a new angle. She felt an encouraging pat on the back. She played her scene from this fresh position and got the comedy over. Next night she had forgotten, but once again the friendly hands guided her; she obeyed and received her applause. From the time she took the position indicated by her unseen helper, she had no more trouble.'

Other actors and actresses struggling with comic roles have had similar experiences. It has been suggested that the ghostly mentor is the spirit of the clown Joseph Grimaldi, who spent many years on the stage of Drury Lane. He was certainly a comic genius and also, according to all accounts, a man of very considerate and generous temperament.

Far less charming is the 'grim and fearsome figure' of Charles Macklin, an Irish actor with a quick temper who, in 1735, got into a row with a fellow thespian over, of all things, a wig. Macklin struck out at his rival with his cane. It caught him in the eye and the blow ultimately proved fatal. From time to time Macklin's ghost has been witnessed marching across the stage, his face set in a mask of remorse.

The interior of the Theatre Royal, Drury Lane, shortly after it re-opened in 1812.

Joseph Grimaldi spent much of his time on the stage at Sadler's Wells Theatre. He first performed here in 1718 when he was just three years old, giving his final performance in 1828. His ghost has been seen in one of the boxes, his white-painted face leering out of the dark as if floating – a nightmare for anyone who doesn't like clowns. On occasions he has made his appearances during a performance, the occupants of the box so intent on what is happening on the stage that they are entirely unaware of the ghostly clown's face grinning behind them.

A very strange tale is told about The Lyceum. A husband and wife were watching a show from one of the boxes when the woman happened to glance down and saw a bizarre and horrifying sight. Staring up at her from the lap of a member of the audience was a severed head! Drawn by his wife's start of amazement, the man caught a glimpse of the head too, before the woman in the stalls covered it with a shawl. At the end of the play, the couple hurried down to the auditorium in the hope of accosting the woman, but they were unable to get through the crowd of exiting theatregoers and they watched, frustrated, as she vanished into the night.

A few years later, the male witness was visiting a stately home in Yorkshire when he happened to notice a portrait of a gentleman in 17th-century dress. Staring out of the frame was the same face he and his wife had seen at The Lyceum. He asked about the man and was told that he was a member of the family who had been beheaded on the orders of Oliver Cromwell during the Civil War. He later learnt that the same family had owned the land upon which The Lyceum now stands. Clearly, it was not an actual severed head he and his wife had seen but the apparition of one. The woman in whose lap it appeared to be lying had presumably been unaware of it and had never seen it – which was probably just as well.

The Lyceum, where a weird incident occurred apparently involving a severed head.
Shutterstock/lapas77

One of my favourite theatrical ghosts is the one said to haunt the Old Vic: the apparition of a wild-eyed woman in a white gown who clutches her chest with bloodstained hands. This dramatic ghost hints at some gory deed from the past but is thought to merely show an actress rehearsing her role as Lady Macbeth! She must have been extraordinarily intent on her role if she succeeded in projecting her performance into the ether.

Another ghostly woman haunts the Wimbledon Theatre. She too is thought to have been an actress but her identity is unknown: she is simply referred to as the 'Grey Lady'. Usually she appears as little more than a human-shaped cloud of mist but has been seen in most parts of the theatre, including the ladies' loos. On one memorable occasion in 1980, the Grey Lady manifested in the manageress's bedroom, floating up from the floor. Her head and shoulders were clearly visible this time but what made her visit especially unwelcome was the maniacal laugh she inflicted on the startled manageress. Still cackling, the ghost continued its upward journey and disappeared through the ceiling.

The ghost of the first manager of the Wimbledon Theatre, J.B. Mulholland, makes appearances from time to time, too, sitting in one of the boxes and quietly watching rehearsals. The elegant form of the original owner of the Noël Coward Theatre (formerly the Albery), Sir Charles Wyndham, has been seen striding purposefully round the playhouse he paid to have built in 1903.

The initials 'FF' painted on the proscenium arch of the Theatre Royal, Stratford East, refer to one of its most celebrated managers, Fred Fredericks. According to tradition, his jovial ghost – a chubby figure in a brown suit – makes his visits from beyond the grave to ensure that his initials haven't been painted over. It's said that should they ever be obscured, calamity will befall the Theatre Royal.

A ghostly woman in a crinoline dress has been encountered drifting up and down the so-called Crimson Staircase in the London Palladium. Like so many others, her identity remains unknown, but it is thought she may date from the time when a private home, Argyll House, stood on the site now occupied the Palladium. Parts of Argyll House were incorporated into the theatre's construction, including, it is thought, this staircase.

The ghost of the Old Vic is not what she seems.
©*Matt Humphrey*

Perhaps the saddest ghostly visitor to a theatre is the First World War soldier who made his appearance during a show at the Coliseum. On October 3, 1918, the young soldier in khaki was seen to walk down the gangway of the circle and take a seat in the second row. A few of his friends recognised him but were unable to find him in the interval. They later learnt that he had died in action at that precise moment. His friends knew that his last happy hours before rejoining his regiment had been spent at the Coliseum and they wondered whether, in his last extremity, his spirit had briefly returned there.

THE HAUNTED THAMES

Dividing the City of London in two is the mighty River Thames. The oldest inhabited areas of the city are alongside its margins and the remains of bridges and other artefacts dating way back into prehistory have been found hidden in its thick mud. For thousands of years the river was the main thoroughfare through London, for it was far quicker to transport people and goods up country or down to the sea by boat than along muddy tracks and roads. The Thames is as important a part of London's history as its many grand old buildings. It too is haunted, and indeed we have already encountered one of its ghosts – Anne Boleyn's barge – but there are many others.

The Pool of London is the busy area of the River Thames between London Bridge and Tower Bridge. Some say that at certain times of the year after dark, distressing cries and screams are heard emanating from the Pool. Tradition has it that the phenomenon recalls a tragedy which took place in the 1200s during one of several pogroms against the Jewish inhabitants of England. Jews were successful merchants and moneylenders, often lending vast amounts to English monarchs to help fund their seemingly endless wars. It therefore became expedient at times to default on the loans and use religious intolerance as an excuse to expel them.

During one such expulsion from London, a large party of Jews took ship with an unscrupulous captain, who convinced them with a ruse to disembark on a mudbank where the Pool is now situated. Then he sailed away, taking with him the Jews' worldly possessions, leaving the men, women and children to drown as the tide came in. It is their pitiful cries for help – which never came – that are said to still be heard.

West of the City, the Albert Bridge connects Battersea with Chelsea. In an article on 'Legends of the Thames' in the July 2010 edition of *Paranormal Magazine*, Robert Goodman recounts a ghost story associated with the Albert Bridge. He writes: 'The following story was told to me by an old River Thames waterman I used to know when I myself worked on the river on the pleasure cruisers. I only ever knew him as Alan, but he had worked on the river all his life.

'Alan told me that back in 1870 or thereabouts, an old wherry (or cargo) boat was passing underneath the bridge when for reasons unknown she caught fire. The fire spread rapidly, with the December wind fanning the flames, and the vessel quickly sank into the freezing waters. For many years it was said that flames could be seen on the surface of the water by the bridge, and the cries of the wherryman and his crew heard as the current dragged them down.'

The Pool of London is a haunted stretch of the River Thames.
Shutterstock/godrick

An even worse tragedy took place towards the opposite end of the river in the same decade and this too is claimed to have created a psychic echo. On the evening of September 3, 1878, a pleasure cruiser called the *Princess Alice* was heading back up river to drop off hundreds of passengers when, just off Tripcock Point, at Beckton, disaster struck. A 1,336-ton steamer loaded with coal was heading in the opposite direction. The tides are notoriously difficult to navigate here, and the ships collided – the heavy collier crashing through the *Princess Alice* and splitting her in two.

Hundreds of people died in the accident, some killed as a direct result of the collision, while many others drowned. A good many initially survived but then succumbed to either diseases they'd picked up in the river or to the cocktail of chemicals they swallowed while in the water. At the time this was one of the most polluted stretches of the River Thames. Again, it is the desperate cries of the drowning (heard on the anniversary of the disaster), rather than any visual ghost, that is now said to haunt the river here.

In contrast, the ghost of Westminster Bridge is seen but not heard. For years there have been reports of a boat which sails silently up to and then under the bridge, but which fails to emerge on the other side. Its identity or even its possible date of origin are unrecorded, however.

A remarkable number of bridges across the Thames are haunted. In folklore, bridges were considered uncanny because they were seen as not quite of this world: by connecting places they had a transitional nature which the paranormal could exploit. The area around the northern end of Blackfriars Bridge is another example. Many years ago a clergyman was passing by this spot when he saw a ghastly scene played out in front of him. He saw two men carrying a headless body, which they then threw into the Thames. There was no audible splash and the men winked out of existence before the clergyman had the chance to react.

Presumably, the witness had seen a visual echo of some past murder. Something similar was seen nearby in the 1830s. At Blackfriars, London's second river, the Fleet, flows into the Thames. The Fleet is now entirely submerged under building development but in the 1830s it was still open to the air. A merchant was returning to his ship when he stumbled upon a woman huddled beside the Fleet. He crouched down to render her assistance. The woman turned to face him and pointed to a bloody gash in her throat – then she vanished.

Railway staff working on Barnes Bridge have occasionally encountered the ghost of an intimidating-looking woman whose face is set in what has been described as an 'extremely forbidding' expression. This is the apparition of Kate Webster, who, in 1879, murdered her employer, a Mrs Thomas of Richmond. After helping herself to Mrs Thomas's belongings, she chopped up her body, put it in a box and dropped it off Barnes Bridge. Webster assumed the box would sink to the bottom or be washed out to sea, taking the evidence with it. But as luck would have it, the box was washed up on a nearby mudbank a few days later. Webster was soon caught, charged and hanged.

Many of London's bridges are haunted, including Westminster Bridge.
Shutterstock/dade72

An equally unpleasant package was found washed up against one of the abutments of Waterloo Bridge during the 19th century. At about 5.30am on October 9, 1857, two lightermen were rowing out to a moored barge when they spotted a carpet bag caught beneath the bridge. On investigating, they discovered to their horror that it contained human body parts. They wasted no time in handing the bag over to the police, who immediately realised that the head, hands and feet of the corpse were missing. These were never recovered and so the identity of the unfortunate man was never established. One theory was that they were the remains of a secret agent who had been infiltrating a gang of Italian revolutionaries in Soho. This habit of cutting up bodies and hiding the most identifiable parts in different places is one that recurs in regards to the Mafia. Ever since the discovery of the corpse, the headless ghost of a man was said to haunt the old Waterloo Bridge.

The present-day Waterloo Bridge was built during the 1940s to replace the water-damaged original of the early 19th century. However, as we have seen in the case of one or two of the haunted theatres, this doesn't necessarily mean that ghosts of an earlier period might not still haunt it. In the 1840s Waterloo Bridge became notorious as a place favoured by suicides. In those days it was a toll bridge and after dark less likely to be populated than the busier Westminster or London Bridges. Many of these suicides were said to linger round the bridge in the form of ghosts.

Elliott O'Donnell recounted a remarkable story dating from shortly after the modern bridge was built. A police constable was approached one foggy night by a hysterical young woman who told him someone was poised to jump off Waterloo Bridge and into the swirling waters below. The policeman hurried on to the bridge, the woman following, as he thought. He was just in time to prevent a woman from leaping from the parapet. As he dragged her back, he was astonished to find that she was identical to the woman who had come to warn him. It was then he realised that the 'other' woman was nowhere to be seen. Somehow, it seemed, the desperate and unhappy woman had projected her own apparition to prevent her death.

Near to Waterloo Bridge is that most unusual of London monuments, Cleopatra's Needle. This Ancient Egyptian obelisk stands on Victoria Embankment with bronze sphinxes at its base. Although it is a genuine artefact (unlike the decorative sphinxes), the monument has nothing to do with Queen Cleopatra, for it was made about a thousand years before her reign. The obelisk was presented to the British people in 1819 by the then Sultan of Egypt and Sudan, Muhammad Ali, in tribute to the victories over Napoleon by Lord Nelson and Sir Ralph Abercromby (in, respectively, the Battle of the Nile and the Battle of Alexandria).

No attempt was made to acquire the gift from Egypt for nearly sixty years. The attempt to transport it in 1877 proved disastrous when the specially designed ship carrying the monument was struck by a storm in the Bay of Biscay. Numerous sailors lost their lives and the ship was left to sink or float as chance would have it. Days later it was rescued and towed to a Spanish port. Cleopatra's Needle finally found its way to London the following year and was erected on the Embankment on September 12, 1878.

A peculiar ghost haunts the steps which lead down to the river below Cleopatra's Needle. This is the figure of a large, naked man who is seen to run down the steps and then dive into the water without making a splash. The apparition may be of another suicide but Elliott O'Donnell's description of the spook suggests something far stranger. He spoke to a down-and-out who had seen it while trying to get some sleep on one of the benches along the Embankment. He told O'Donnell that the figure had 'a peak-shaped head and a body covered in what looked like scales'.

For many years Waterloo Bridge had the unenviable reputation as the most popular place in London to commit suicide.
Shutterstock/r.nagy

Finally, we consider what goes on – or has gone on – *beneath* the River Thames. In 1968 a tunnel was being constructed under the Thames near Vauxhall Bridge in order to accommodate a stretch of the Underground Victoria Line. Workmen in the tunnel saw a huge figure of a man, which the Irish 'navvies' soon christened the 'Quare Feller'. One of those who saw the Quare Feller was 'Big Lou' Chalmers. Mr Chalmers told the Press: 'I served in the paratroops in World War II but I've never been so scared since I came across this Thing. There I was working alone when I felt something brush against the back of my neck. I turned round and there it was, the shape of a man about seven feet tall with arms outstretched as if reaching to get hold of something. I didn't stop to take in the details. I just ran.'

A navvy who was able to observe the ghost at a distance of 25 yards noticed that it appeared to be wearing a long brown overcoat and a cap. No explanation has ever been made as to the identity of the ghost or why it should be haunting a tunnel deep beneath the river. The cut was entirely new and no fatalities took place during the work.

A so-called 'phantom hitch-hiker' haunts the Blackwall Tunnel. A number of motorists have reported picking up a young man hitching a lift at the northern end of the Tunnel only to find that, halfway through, he has mysteriously vanished from the passenger seat. The most remarkable occasion was when a motorcyclist gave a lift to the hitch-hiker. The young man asked if he could be taken to an address in Essex. This was agreed, so the hitch-hiker donned the biker's spare helmet and got up behind him. When the bike emerged from the Tunnel, however, the motorcyclist found that his pillion passenger had gone, although he could not have fallen off without certainly causing the cars behind to crash. The spare helmet was still tied in its usual place.

Greatly puzzled and a little frightened, the biker decided to continue to the address the hitch-hiker had given him. Here he was shocked to learn that the young man had died some years before – while riding pillion on a motorbike through the Blackwall Tunnel!

(It should be pointed out that there are many versions of the above story told about a number of locations in the British Isles. It is a modern folk tale.)

JACK THE RIPPER'S EAST END

In 1888 five gruesome murders took place in and around Whitechapel. Common factors in the killings were that the victims were all prostitutes and that, after their throats were cut, the women's abdomens were mutilated. In three cases, body parts were removed, leading to the suggestion that the murderer might be a doctor or a surgeon. When a news agency received a letter purportedly written by the killer and signed 'Jack the Ripper', a legend was born.

A number of other brutal murders took place in broadly the same area up to 1891, some of which may have been by the same perpetrator. It isn't absolutely certain there was only one killer: the letter may have been a hoax. So, too, may have been a follow-up letter. In the minds of the public and the Press, however, one man was responsible: Jack the Ripper. No one was ever brought to trial for the murders, so we will never know.

Of the five likely to have been carried out by the one man – the Ripper – the first murder took place on August 31, 1888, in Durward Street (formerly Buck's Row), Whitechapel. The body of Mary Ann Nichols, a 42-year-old prostitute, was found huddled up in the gutter with its throat cut 'almost from ear to ear' and the abdomen wounded by several frenzied slashes. According to Elliott O'Donnell, 'appalling screams and groans uttered by no living human being' have been heard in Durward Street after dark and the apparition of Nichols's corpse has been seen lying in the gutter, illuminated by a weird phosphorescent glow.

A week later, on September 8, Jack the Ripper struck again. His second victim was Annie Chapman, aged 47. She was killed in Hanbury Street, Spitalfields. Her throat had been gashed twice by deep cuts and her abdomen had been sliced open. An examination later showed that her uterus had been removed. At 5.30am a witness had seen Chapman with a man of 'shabby genteel appearance', possibly the only genuine sighting of Jack the Ripper. Half an hour later the woman's body was found in the yard of 29 Hanbury Street.

The location is now occupied by the Truman Brewery building, long since converted into offices. At about 6am on the anniversary of the murder, a strange chill has been known to descend on the occupants of this building. The unfortunate woman's ghost has also been seen in one of the storerooms.

While researching a book on Jack the Ripper, veteran ghost-hunter Peter Underwood learnt of further apparitions that might be linked to the murder of Annie Chapman. The sightings were both made in the years before the brewery was built. On a number of occasions during the 1930s a man living opposite saw the phantoms of a woman in a long skirt and a man in a dark overcoat and wide-brimmed hat walk through the solid door into the yard of 29 Hanbury Street without opening it. On another occasion he passed them in the street. Quickly turning to get a better look at them, he found they had vanished. The witness's name was a Mr

Chapman – is this a coincidence, or was he in fact related to the murdered woman, providing him with a psychic link to her last moments on earth?

Mr Underwood spoke to another Hanbury Street resident who may have heard a ghostly echo of the murder, although nothing visible became apparent. The witness described hearing muffled voices, heavy breathing and the sounds of a struggle from behind the fence round No. 29's backyard. He jumped up and peered over the fence to see what was going on but to his amazement the yard was deserted. Nonetheless, he then heard a dull thump and the sound of something heavy being dragged across the empty yard. Now thoroughly spooked, he decided to investigate no further and hurried on his way.

An old East End of London street after dark. The ghostly echoes of Jack the Ripper's foul crimes are said to still be experienced in the streets where they were carried out.
Shutterstock/Bartlomiej Nowak

The Ripper's third victim was a Swede named Elizabeth Stride. Her body was found in an open space between a warehouse and a disused stables in Henriques Street (formerly Berner Street), Whitechapel. Elliott O'Donnell claims that here too ghostly 'moaning and groaning' marked the place where the murder was committed years after the event.

The fourth and fifth women to suffer at the Ripper's hands were Catherine Eddowes and Mary Jane Kelly. Their ghosts also continued to haunt the locations of their deaths, according to author James Clark. In his *Haunted London*, Mr Clark relates how the shadowy form of Eddowes's corpse is still to be seen from time to time in Mitre Square, Aldgate, where it originally lay on September 30, 1888. The appearances, in the south corner of the little square, are more frequent in September than at any other time.

Mary Jane Kelly was the only one of Jack the Ripper's victims to be killed indoors. Like the others, she worked as a prostitute and it seems that she must have brought the killer home with her. Her lodgings were in Dorset Street, Spitalfields, once described as 'the worst street in London' because of its run-down buildings and high crime rate. Kelly had often voiced her fear of encountering the Ripper but a desperate shortage of money forced her out to solicit again on the night of the Lord Mayor's Show (November 9, 1888), when plenty of clients might be anticipated. Tragically, she chose very much the wrong one. In the seclusion of Kelly's little room, the Ripper had more time to carry out his insane desires. The woman's body was the most mutilated of all.

After her murder, many people claimed to have seen Mary Kelly's ghost in Dover Street. She was always dressed in black. A neighbour, Mrs Maxwell, stated in evidence that she had twice seen Mary Kelly and spoken to her on the morning of November 9, hours after she had died. The police put this down to mistaken identity but perhaps there was a supernatural explanation. Many years later, a woman who moved into the rooms once occupied by Mary Kelly claimed that she discovered a bloody hand-print behind a picture of the Crucifixion and that, however hard she tried, it would not wash off. Dorset Street no longer exists. It was demolished to make way for redevelopment of Spitalfields Market.

The Ten Bells pub in nearby Commercial Street was, for a time, renamed The Jack the Ripper. Mary Kelly was last seen alive waving a cheery farewell as she left the Ten Bells to begin plying her trade. For a while, staff feared that the apparition of an old man dressed in clothing of the Victorian period might be the ghost of the Ripper himself. It had the habit of chuckling in a sinister fashion behind half-opened doors. More unnerving still, live-in employees would sometimes wake up to find the ghost stretched out beside them on their beds! It would vanish as soon as they cried out.

A chance discovery in the cellar showed that the phantom was more likely to be of a former landlord than of the notorious murderer. A metal box tucked away in a dark corner was found to contain the personal effects of one George Roberts, who had been landlord of the Ten Bells in the early 1900s.

The box also contained a faded newspaper report revealing that Mr Roberts was in fact the victim of murder: he was axed to death in a Swansea cinema.

Another grim discovery was later made in the pub, when a sack stuffed behind a water tank was found to contain mouldy and bloodstained baby clothes. A few years previously, a psychic visiting the pub had become overwhelmed with a feeling of horror outside one of the bedrooms. She refused to go in, saying that she had the violent impression of the brutal murder of a baby in the room. The baby clothes were found in the roof space directly above that room.

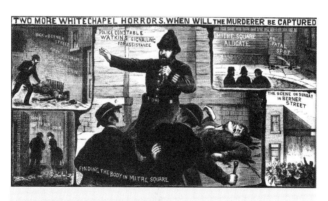

An illustration from The London Police News detailing the horrors of Jack the Ripper's activities. The south corner of Mitre Square, pictured top right, is one of the places said to have become haunted after the murder committed there.

MORE NOTABLE HAUNTS

No book of this size could hope to include in any detail all the haunted locations in London – indeed it would take several volumes – but in this closing chapter I will endeavour to cover a few more of the most interesting.

Certainly one of the capital's grandest and most unexpected buildings to have a haunted reputation is the Bank of England. 'The Old Lady of Threadneedle Street' was at one time visited by a ghostly old lady. In life she was Sarah Whitehead, whose brother Phillip was a clerk at the Bank. In 1811 Phillip was convicted of forgery and hanged for his crime. He managed to keep his disgrace from his sister, so she had no idea why she had not heard from him for such a long time. Eventually, her letters remaining unanswered, she visited his place of work to ask after him. Embarrassed members of staff initially fobbed off the worried woman but she refused to be put off and on a third or fourth visit to the Bank, a young clerk blurted out the truth. Poor Sarah was so shocked that she became demented and had to be restrained.

The thought of her brother's lonely disgrace and execution preyed on Sarah's mind and finally turned it. For twenty-five years she would make daily visits to the Bank of England, asking after her brother. Fearing a repeat of another breakdown, the employees were all under instructions to simply tell her that Phillip was ill and not working that day.

Sarah would accept this lie and meekly leave the building. But she would always be back the next day. Sarah eventually wore herself to death but this did not stop her repeated visits to the Bank; only this time she would come in ghostly form. Her ghost was encountered on the street leading to the Bank and in the Bank itself.

Some say Sarah Whitehead's ghost was also seen in the private garden behind the Bank of England. One source states that the garden was formerly part of the grounds of the Church of St Christopher-le-Stocks, where Sarah was buried. However, the ghost of the garden was generally referred to as 'The Black Nun'. Despite her confusion over her brother's death, Sarah would always wear deep mourning, and it's possible that a woman in black Victorian clothing could be mistaken for a nun. It's also possible that the Nun is a different ghost altogether, dating from an earlier time.

Another, rather more fearsome-looking phantom haunts the garden of the Bank of England. This is the gigantic but benign spirit of a former cashier who had stood almost eight feet tall, with a bulk to match. He was a wonder to the customers and a useful chap to have around the place but he had a secret dread. He lived in the years when 'resurrectionists' were rife in London, men who would dig up freshly interred corpses and sell them to doctors for use in dissections and medical experiments. Recognising that his unusual stature would be of interest to anatomists, he feared becoming a target of grave-robbers after his death. He begged his managers to allow his body to be buried in the garden. Where in London could be safer from robbers than the Bank of England? His wish was granted but after his burial (which may have been in unconsecrated ground) the small regiment of soldiers who guarded the Bank often reported seeing his eight-foot-tall ghost looming out of the darkness at them.

The Bank of England is the surprising haunt of a number of ghosts.
Shutterstock/alessandro0770

Walpole House on Chiswick Mall alongside the Thames is one of the finest private residences in London. It is the former home of Sir Thomas Walpole (after whom it is named) and before him the Duchess of Cleveland. The 17th-century house also featured in Thackeray's *Vanity Fair* as Miss Pinkerton's

Academy for Young Ladies. However, it is Barbara Villiers, Duchess of Cleveland, whom we are concerned with here. Barbara was one of the mistresses of King Charles II and bore him five illegitimate sons. It is for this reason that she was made a duchess. Charles Harper describes her as 'the most completely depraved of a dissolute number of women whose accommodating lack of morals was the scandal of even that easy age', but this is a rather Victorian viewpoint.

King Charles was loyal to Barbara Villiers for longer than most of his many women but it is the lot of royal mistresses to become abandoned after a certain age. Once her looks had begun to fade, the newly honoured Duchess of Cleveland was pensioned off to Walpole House and a rather lonely retirement. Into her old age, Barbara began to suffer the worst fate a vain woman can endure: not only was she no longer pretty, but her looks began to grow distorted and grotesque. She was suffering from dropsy, a condition which made her face and body swell to monstrous proportions. The lonesome unhappy woman shut herself off from society, too ashamed to be seen.

Occasionally she would be glimpsed peering out of an upper storey window on nights when the moon was bright but when she hoped she might not be observed. And this was how Barbara – or rather her apparition – was still occasionally to be seen for years after her death in 1709. On moonlit, but stormy nights, 'with cloud-wracks scudding across the sky' (as Harper romantically puts it), the ghost of Barbara Villiers would manifest at a window, a grotesquely bloated woman, wringing her hands and entreating heaven: 'Give me back my lost beauty!'

Not far away is Chiswick House, a stylish mansion built by the Earl of Burlington in 1729 to show off his art collection and to use for parties (those were the days!). The house and its award-winning gardens are open to the public. The ghost researcher Andrew Green had an extraordinary experience at Chiswick House during a period of renovation in the 1960s. Walking round early one afternoon, the appetising smell of bacon and eggs accosted his nostrils and he jokingly asked of one of the workmen who it was enjoying a late breakfast. He was told that 'the ghost of one of the mad cooks' was responsible.

'In fact,' explains Green in his book *Our Haunted Kingdom*, 'the smell of cooking breakfast foods has been noticed by a lot of people over a long period.'

The then head custodian told Green that the aroma had been noticed at irregular intervals, despite the fact that no one had cooked food at Chiswick House for more than a century. The aroma tended to be detected near the north wing, where the kitchens were originally situated. Today there is a café, so it's possible that if the ghostly aroma manifests again it will simply go unnoticed.

The art deco splendour of the BBC's Broadcasting House also hosts a rather unexpected ghost. This is the apparition of a butler, in black tie and jacket, steadily pacing a fourth-floor corridor and carrying before him a laden silver tray. Many reliable witnesses saw the phantom butler in the years before World War II. One member of staff who followed him down the corridor without realising he was a ghost particularly noticed that he walked with a limp and that he had a hole in the heel of his left sock. Clearly, he dates from that magic period when even newsreaders wore black tie and guests could expect a five-star service from the Beeb.

Chiswick House is haunted by a ghostly aroma.
Shutterstock/Kiev.Victor

Bruce Castle, Tottenham, is a rare survivor of a Tudor manor house in the heart of London. One of the oldest brick-built houses in England, it is now a museum. A chilling phenomenon is said to take place every November 3 at Bruce Castle. On that date in 1680, Constantia, wife of the insane

Lord Coleraine, threw herself to her death. The crazily possessive Lord Coleraine had Constantia locked up in the tiny room under the clock. Finally, she could stand her imprisonment no longer and, her baby clasped in her arms, she hurled herself over the balustrade. Tradition states that her screaming ghost repeats the tragedy on the anniversary of her death.

On a number of occasions a ghostly group of about a dozen people dressed in the fashions of the 18th century have been observed just outside Bruce Castle's main entrance. They appear to be thoroughly enjoying themselves but do so in total silence.

London has very many haunted pubs but I only have room here to mention one. The most famously haunted ale-house is certainly the Grenadier in Wilton Row. In the early 1800s the Grenadier was used as a kind of mess by the Duke of Wellington's regiment (the Duke himself lived nearby at Apsley House). One fateful night a young officer accused of cheating at cards met a violent end; possibly he was flogged to death. It is his ghost that haunts the Grenadier. The soldier's shadowy figure has been seen climbing the back stairs but the haunting is often more intangible, an atmosphere of menace which one previous landlord said even his dogs noticed, as they growled and snarled at unseen things. The haunting is most severe in September, because this is the month in which the soldier died.

On the anniversary of her death, the ghost of Constantia, Lady Coleraine, is seen to fall from the balustrade on the clock tower of Bruce Castle.
Shutterstock/Kiev.Victor

A number of ghosts have been reported from the complex of grand 18th-century buildings at Greenwich. Over the years numerous members of staff have noticed strange goings-on at the Queen Anne Block of the Royal Naval College. Shuffling footsteps are heard in the passage-ways and doors are opened and closed by invisible hands. Occasionally misty shapes have been glimpsed or, more substantially, an apparition described as 'a shrouded figure'. These are put down to the brooding, ghostly presence of Admiral Byng, who was imprisoned in a small room in the building in the 1750s. Byng was unfairly found guilty of treason after a failed naval battle and was later shot by firing squad on board his own ship.

Disembodied footsteps were also heard in the Queen's House, the palatial mansion designed by celebrated architect Inigo Jones for the use of Henrietta Maria, the unhappy wife of gadabout Charles I. The footsteps were heard during a paranormal investigation carried out by the Ghost Club. The Ghost Club had been inspired to investigate the Queen's House after a remarkable photograph was taken in 1966 by a member of the public. The Revd Hardy took a long exposure of the elegant Tulip Staircase in the house only to find, on being developed, that it showed a hand sliding up the banister, with a ring on one finger and the arm clad in loose white material. The photograph has never satisfactorily been explained.

Tudor buildings originally stood on the site now occupied by the Royal Naval College. Henry VIII was born in a palace at Greenwich. However, it is the ghost of Henry's daughter, Queen Elizabeth I, which is said to walk around the grounds of the Queen's House.

Also at Greenwich can be found *Cutty Sark*, one of the world's last and fastest tea clippers, now permanently moored as a museum. *Cutty Sark* is one of London's more unusual haunted locations. The apparition of a sailor, scanning some far horizon, is said to be seen perched high up in the rigging. He is thought to be the ghost of one of the crewmen who died in a storm which struck *Cutty Sark* off the coast of Cape Horn.

Once upon a time, London's most famous haunted house was 50 Berkeley Square, in the City of Westminster. Originally a private residence, owned for many years by Prime Minister George Canning, it became the home of antiquarian booksellers Maggs Brothers in the 1930s and it remains so today.

The legends of 50 Berkeley Square are numerous. The most persistent is that it was haunted by something so dreadful that it could frighten people to death. One story refers to a maid who is instructed to open up the unused 'haunted room' and who goes mad as the result of something she sees there. The guest, a military man, who was to be given the room, learns of the incident but refuses to be put off. He insists on sleeping in the room but as a precaution takes his gun to bed with him and also a bell. He says that if he rings the bell, the rest of the house should ignore it, because he might ring it out of sheer nerves. If he rings it a second time, though, they should assume he needs help. Just after midnight, the bell rings. Those who have stayed up pause in their flight to his assistance but when it frantically rings a second time, they all hurry along to the haunted bedroom. Bursting in, they find the military man dead, his face fixed in a mask of terror.

'The Truth, The Whole Truth and Nothing but the Truth', a short story by the now largely forgotten Victorian novelist Rhoda Broughton, bears remarkable similarities to this yarn. Although she suppresses the location and names of those involved, Broughton insists at its conclusion, 'This is a true

Queen's House, Greenwich, where a classic photograph of a ghost was taken.
Shutterstock/Alan Jeffery

story' (one would have thought its lengthy title would have already made that clear!). Other commentators have noted similarities between the alleged goings-on at 50 Berkeley Square and Edward Bulwer-Lytton's better-known tale 'The Haunted and the Haunters'.

Further startling stories have been told about this rather elegant Georgian townhouse. Peter Underwood, in his *Haunted London*, tells of two sailors who, looking for somewhere to crash, notice the 'For Sale' sign outside 50 Berkeley Square and decide to break in. This was during a period in which the house had been abandoned to its ghosts, but of course the sailors did not know that. They spent a terrifying night, kept awake by bangs and crashes, doors slamming and, worst of all, footsteps 'that seemed to slither and slide' towards the door of the attic room in which they had bedded down. After several hours of this, the door opened and an indescribable shapeless mass of horror oozed into the room. The thing emanated an atmosphere of such evil that one of the seamen, in blind panic, threw himself out of the window. He met his death on the iron railings below. The other man dived past the monstrosity and lived to tell his tale.

So, what caused the intense haunting at 50 Berkeley Square? Again, there are a number of explanations. One is that centuries ago a young woman threw herself from the attic window in order to escape the clutches of a lustful uncle. Another is that a dangerous lunatic was kept locked away in the attic and fed through a hatch in the door, going steadily more crazed with every passing year. Then there is the theory about a Mr Myers, who bought the house and spent thousands of pounds decorating it for his much younger bride. When she jilted him at the altar, he shut himself away in it and brooded into insanity, Miss Haversham-like. In each version, the unfortunate person's vengeful spirit returned to wreak havoc. Jessie Middleton (in *The Grey Ghost Book*) refers to a little girl who was frightened to death by something in the house and then haunted it herself. This is possibly the only account of one ghost generating another.

Most sources state that all has been quiet – in the paranormal sense – at 50 Berkeley Square for a long time but Richard Jones, who has been running ghost tours round London for

Formerly London's most haunted house, 50 Berkeley Square, sketched by Charles Harper in the early 1900s.

years, spoke directly to employees at Maggs Brothers and
learnt that spooky things do occasionally still take place. In his
Haunted London, he writes:

'A bookseller with Maggs Brothers was working alone in the
accounts department, which now occupies the haunted room.
Suddenly, a column of brown mist moved quickly across the
room and vanished. Another man was shocked when his
glasses were snatched from his hand and flung to the ground
as he was walking up the stairs.'

Before we leave London, there is just room to mention another
of its best-known haunts: the extensive and historic cemetery
in Highgate. A Grade I-listed location, Highgate Cemetery
opened in 1839 and became one of the most fashionable
places for well-off Londoners to bury their loved ones.
Grandiose monuments became the norm, making it a focus
for enthusiasts of the Gothic. The eastern part is the oldest
and most elaborate, and the tombs of its most famous
'residents' are to be found here, including Karl Marx, George
Eliot, Douglas Adams, Anthony Shaffer and Ralph
Richardson. This section of the cemetery is only accessible as
part of an organised tour but the rest is generally open for the
public to stroll around at their leisure.

Highgate Cemetery became the centre of a vampire scare in
the 1970s but many consider the debacle to have been a hoax.
Nevertheless, there are persistent reports of ghostly figures
seen in and around the cemetery by both locals and ghost-
hunters. These include a melancholy man with 'bony fingers',

a gaunt figure with a 'horrific expression' and a woman frantically searching for the graves of the children she murdered. Rather more cheerful is the phantom of a man in a cape, riding an old-fashioned bicycle, who glides down the lane leading past the cemetery.

Highgate Cemetery is without doubt one of the most atmospheric places to visit in a city overly blessed – or cursed – with historic haunted locations.

Highgate Cemetery is one of London's most atmospheric haunted locations.
Shutterstock/Don Cline